THE BATTLE OF KURSK

Hitler vs. The Red Army

Written by Jonathan Duhoux
In collaboration with Thomas Jacquemin
Translated by Carly Probert

History   50MINUTES.com

THE BATTLE OF KURSK

KEY INFORMATION

- **When:** 5 July - 23 August 1943
- **Where:** In the neighborhood of Kursk (Russia)
- **Context:** The Second World War (1939-1945)
- **Belligerents:** The Third Reich against The Union of Soviet Socialist Republics (USSR)
- **Commanders and leaders:**
    - Erich von Manstein, German general (1887-1973)
    - Walter Model, German general (1891-1945)
    - Nicolai Fyodorovich Vatutin, Russian general (1901-1944)
    - Jukov, Russian general (1896-1974)
- **Outcome:** Russian victory
- **Victims:**
    - Russian camp: approximately 200 000 killed, 660 000 wounded and missing
    - German camp: approximately 90 000 killed, 400 000 wounded and missing

INTRODUCTION

Although less well-known than the Battle of Stalingrad (September 1942-February 1943), Kursk was nevertheless one of the main confrontations between the Germans and the Russians during the Second World War and one of the most significant tank battles in history.

The offensive was launched by Germany in July 1943 under

the name Operation Citadel. The goal was to regain the initiative on the Eastern Front after the major defeat they had undergone in Stalingrad. Adolf Hitler (1889-1945) hoped to be able to seize the territories they had lost during the winter, relying on the fact that the *Wehrmacht* (German army) had always proved itself to be superior under favorable climatic conditions.

In order to obtain a victory that would forever be remembered, Germany aligned an impressive fighting force on the Kursk salient (a salient of 23 000 km^2, located between Orel in the North and Belgorod in the South, which ran into the German front): There were roughly one million soldiers, more than 2 500 tanks and 2 000 planes on the front. However, the operation was delayed and the Red Army, informed of the operation, had time to prepare. Consequently, when the battle broke out, the Soviets were able to count on a numerically superior army of 1.3 million men, 3 600 tanks and 200 planes. After more than a month of fighting, the German troops were pushed back, at a heavy cost for both armies. This defeat meant the end of the Führer's last hopes to vanquish the Soviet Union.

POLITICAL AND SOCIAL CONTEXT

The battle of Kursk took place in the context of the Second World War, which militarily opposed:

- the Axis, with Germany, Italy and Japan;
- the Allies, with the United States, the United Kingdom and the Soviet Union.

THE ORIGINS OF THE SECOND WORLD WAR

Although it was a result of World War I (1914-1918), World War II was very different. The motivations, the belligerents and the social context had greatly changed during the two decades separating the two conflicts.

Many factors contributed to the creation of an explosive situation in 1939, including:

- The consequences of the Treaty of Versailles, which aimed to re-establish peace and define the punishments to be paid by Germany, which was considered to be responsible for this first world conflict. While the winning countries wanted a strict enforcement of the treaty ratified at the end of the First World War, others would have liked it to be revised. This was namely the case with Germany, whose war debts were enormous, and Italy, who was among the winners but couldn't expand its territory, as opposed to the other European powers.
- The economic crisis. From 1929, the unemployment rate rose drastically in many countries, which became inwar-

dly focused. The people, ruined, were ready for change, thus constituting a very favorable ground for extremism.

- The German expansionist policy. In his book Mein Kampf (1923-1924), Adolf Hitler explained his desire to expand Germany, a desire which he justified through the population growth of his country and his duty to offer his people a territory big enough for its needs.
- Italian expansionism. Benito Mussolini (Italian statesman, 1883-1945) also wished to expand the territory of his country. Therefore, he conquered Ethiopia in 1936 and Albania in 1939. That same year, he signed a German-Italian military alliance called the Pact of Steel;
- The arms race. From 1933, Adolf Hitler increased the military strength of Germany, despite the interdiction imposed by the Treaty of Versailles.
- The Spanish Civil War (1936-1939). General Francisco Franco (1892-1975) tried to overthrow the democratic government in place and was supported in this by Adolf Hitler and Benito Mussolini.

> best representatives of this Aryan race;
> * A totalitarian state, led by an almighty leader, is necessary for the flourishing of the German race when facing the people he judged to be inferior.
>
> Adolf Hitler took advantage of the difficult social and economic context to impose his ideas on the population. After his rise to power in 1933, he progressively imposed the Nazi ideology on Germany and established the Third Reich. This ideology would later die along with the Führer, in May 1945.

Europe seemed to catch fire, but France and the United Kingdom remained relatively passive in the face of all these early warning signs, thus allowing Adolf Hitler to plan his conquest. He first invaded Austria in 1938 (the *Anschluss*) and received a warning from the Allies during the Munich conference that same year, after he attacked Czechoslovakia. But it was not until the month of September 1939 and the beginning of the invasion of Poland that France and the UK declared war on Germany.

TREATY OF NON-AGGRESSION BETWEEN GERMANY AND THE USSR

Adolf Hitler managed to invade Poland in 1939 due to the fact that he had concluded an agreement with the Russian giant. The treaty of non-aggression between Germany and the Soviet Union ensured the neutrality of one of the two countries if the other were to be at war. But this agreement also included a secret clause: the repartition of the Eastern European countries among the Führer and Joseph Stalin (Soviet statesman, 1878-1953). According to the terms of this pact, Poland was to be divided between Germany and the Soviet Union.

Such a treaty surprised the whole of Europe because of the differences existing between the two political systems and because of the lack of common interests. But, in reality, Joseph Stalin feared the German power and didn't trust the European democracies to help him. He even suspected France and the UK of encouraging Germany to attack Russia in order to get rid of the threat of communism.

and developed the economy through collectivization and planning, which came closer to an oligarchy, or even a dictatorship. Little by little, the USSR tried to convert the whole world to its ideology – through the Internationals –, which considerably worried the European democracies.

The *Wehrmacht* crossed the Polish border on 1 September 1939. France and the UK immediately declared war on Adolf Hitler, but didn't intervene militarily. On 17 September, the Russians entered Poland and finalized the sharing of the country with Germany on 28 September.

From then on, in Western Europe, all the armies stood in their positions until spring, in what would later be called 'the phony war'. During this period, the Germans and the French faced each other along the border, but didn't attempt anything. Tensions were growing, but thanks to the treaty of non-aggression, Adolf Hitler knew that his dangerous Eastern adversary would not intervene. The Führer was therefore free to focus all his armed forces in Western Europe.

In the spring of 1940, the Germans opened five successive front lines and used the technique known as *Blitzkrieg* (meaning "lightning war"), which consisted of associating land, air and mechanical forces in a well-defined sector in order to destroy the enemy defenses in a very short time. The *Wehrmacht* achieved victory after victory:

- Denmark was invaded on 9 April and capitulated on the

same day;
- Norway was invaded on 9 April and capitulated on the 10 June;
- Belgium was invaded on 10 May and capitulated on 28 May;
- The Netherlands was invaded on 10 May and capitulated on 25 June;
- France was invaded on 10 May and capitulated on 25 June.

OPERATION BARBAROSSA

But Adolf Hitler did not stop at Western Europe, where only the UK was still resisting. The Führer also wished to expand his vital space toward the East by attacking the Slavs and thus become the master of the oil resources in the Caucasus. On 22 June 1941, he launched Operation Barbarossa, which aimed to invade the USSR, thus marking the end of the German-Soviet Pact.

DID YOU KNOW?

To Adolf Hitler, attacking the USSR was a necessity to abolish communism and to annihilate the Russian Jews who were, according to him, at the heart of the State. This form of ideological and racial crusade was called *Weltanschauungskrieg* by the Germans, i.e. worldview warfare. The Nazi terminology remained vague, however, when it came to distinguishing the Jews from the rest of the Russian population. Thus, the SS leader in charge of the center of Russia, Erich von dem Bach-Zelewski (1899-1972), claimed as soon as

The goal of the German staff was to reach the Kremlin as quickly as possible to have this fortress which housed the Soviet power surrender. Adolf Hitler, however, wished to take Leningrad (now St. Petersburg) and Kronstadt (a Russian harbor) before Moscow. Finally, the attack was split over a front line of several thousands of kilometers, according to three axes:

- In the north, an army moved towards Leningrad through the Baltic countries;
- At the center, the most important strength moved towards Moscow, sending reinforcement to the other armies when necessary;
- In the south, the *Wehrmacht* aimed for the city of Kiev, the harbor of Odessa, then Stalingrad, a strategic location for controlling the Volga (river irrigating more than a third of Russia).

On the Russian side, the generals quickly realized that a war with the Third Reich could not be avoided. But in 1941, Joseph Stalin thought that the concentration of German troops on the Russian borders was a provocation strategy. Operation Barbarossa therefore benefitted from a certain surprise effect, which prevented an efficient Soviet counter-attack. Not as well-equipped and less organized, the Red Army withdrew on every front, until the Battle of Moscow (beginning

1942).

STALINGRAD, THE SYMBOL OF THE GREAT PATRIOTIC WAR

The Soviet Union waged total war to push back the invader. The whole population took part in the war effort and Soviet industrial production increased drastically. The acts of extreme violence perpetrated by the German troops rallied the population around Joseph Stalin who declared 'The Great Patriotic War' on 10 October 1941.

However, by 1942, the military situation had become caught in a dead end on the Eastern Front. The *Wehrmacht* was stuck in front of Leningrad, where it settled for a two-and-a-half-year long siege. In the south, the Battle of Stalingrad was getting bogged down in street fights. It was only during the month of February 1943 that the armed conflicted evolved in a significant way. After five months of bitter conflict, the Soviets managed to push back the *Wehrmacht* from the city. After their surrender, more than 94 000 German soldiers were taken prisoner. The Soviet Union, encouraged by this victory, started the slow reclamation of is territory. But one more major obstacle was lying in its way: the Battle of Kursk.

COMMANDERS AND LEADERS

ERICH VON MANSTEIN, GERMAN GENERAL

Born in 1887, Erich von Manstein, who came from a family of many generals, was predestined to join the German army. He enrolled at the Military Academy in 1913, but his training was interrupted by the First World War, during which he fought in Belgium, Poland and France. He took part in the Battle of Verdun (February-December 1916) and the Battle of the Somme (July-November 1916), and was awarded several military honors.

During the interwar period, he became a fervent anti-communist and therefore rejoiced in Adolf Hitler's rise to power. When the Führer decided to re-arm Germany, thus violating the Treaty of Versailles, Erich von Manstein participated actively in the project. He quickly became second-in-command in the staff of the *Wehrmacht* and perfected the technique of *Blitzkrieg*. After his intervention in the annexation of Austria, Erich von Manstein took part in the Poland Campaign. He then drew up a plan for the invasion of France, which was followed broadly by the German Chancellor.

In 1941, he took part in Operation Barbarossa during which he gained many significant victories. Nevertheless, he was stopped before Leningrad and failed in several rescue attempts during the Battle of Stalingrad. The German general then won the Battle of Kharkov, before preparing for the Operation Citadel.

In charge of the armed forces that were to attack Kursk from the south, Erich von Manstein's mission was to catch the Russians along with generals Walter Model and Hand Günther von Kluge (1882-1944). The offensive began on 5 July 1943. Thinking that the Soviets would lead a counter-attack sooner or later, Erich von Manstein kept many troops as reserves, but he underestimated the size of the enemy's forces and their amount of reinforcements. After one week, Operation Citadel got stuck, before the Germans were forced to retreat. According to the German general, this defeat was due to the many delays in the operation, which had allowed the Soviets to prepare their defenses.

In 1944, Erich von Manstein had to undergo an operation for an eye-problem and subsequently retired. However, until the end, he remained convinced that Nazi Germany could win against the Allies.

In 1949, he was sentenced to 18 years of reclusion for war crimes, but was released four years later for health reasons. He then wrote his memoirs, in which he blamed Hitler for the war and everything it entailed. He died in 1973.

WALTER MODEL, GERMAN GENERAL

The son of a music teacher, Walter Model enrolled at the cadet school in 1908. During his military career, the German general made very few friends, given his ambition and antisocial character. During the First World War, he distinguished himself through his actions, and, despite his bad character, he rose through the ranks. His appointment to the General Staff allowed him to escape the Battle of the

Somme. At the end of the war, he was awarded the rank of captain.

The interwar period allowed him to strengthen his reputation. During that period, he gave strategy lessons to young officers and supported the modernization of the German army. When Nazism took root in the country, he became a fervent supporter.

At the beginning of the Second World War, Walter Model accumulated victories, first in Poland, then in France. When Operation Barbarossa was launched, he led the 3rd Panzer Division at breakneck speed through the Soviet territory.

In 1943, he was put in charge of Operation Citadel, along with Erich von Manstein and Günther von Kluge, in order to avenge the terrible defeat of Stalingrad. Walter Model took charge of the armies attacking the northern flank of the Kursk salient. However, he uttered some doubts as to the success of the operation, given the extent of the Russian defenses. Consequently, the general asked that the operation be delayed in order to consolidate his troops with new tank models, namely the *Jagdpanzer Elefant*, fearsome panzer hunters. But despite technological superiority, the German general, trapped from the beginning of the attack, would never manage to gain the upper hand.

After the defeat of Kursk, Walter Model inflicted heavy losses on the Soviets during their recapture, to which he owed his promotion to the rank of field marshal. In 1944, he was sent to Normandy, where he was forced to gradually withdraw to Germany. When the situation became desperate, at the end of the war, he dissolved his army rather than surrendering. In the end, he committed suicide in April 1945 to avoid being put on trial by the Soviets.

NICOLAI FYODOROVICH VATUTIN, RUSSIAN GENERAL

Born in 1901, Nikolai Fyodorovich Vatutin joined the Red Army in 1920. He quickly became a member of the Communist party to which he devoted himself with passion. In 1940, Joseph Stalin promoted him to the rank of general, but Nicolai Fyodorovich Vatutin lacked experience. He did not manage to stop Operation Barbarossa in 1941.

Nevertheless, he learned from his mistakes and organized several daring maneuvers which allowed him to reverse the course of war. He delayed the German general Erich von Manstein on the northern front, which allowed him to save Leningrad. In the south, he directed the Soviet counter-attack of 1942 on Stalingrad and managed to surround the 6th German Army. He then annihilated the 8th Italian Army which had come to the rescue.

After Stalingrad, he faced Erich von Manstein once more in Kharkov but, taken by surprise, lost the city. The Russian general was nevertheless rewarded by Stalin for his audacity. Promoted to general, he organized the defense of Kursk, where he was supported by other Soviet war heroes, such as Gueorgui Konstantinovitch Jukov and Konstantine Konstantinovitch Rokossovski (1896-1968). Nicolai Fyodorovich Vatutin proved to be tactically creative, which enabled him to push back Erich von Manstein and his allies, despite the technological superiority of the Germans. He gained his advantage by switching directly to the attack, which the German generals had not foreseen. He then undertook the slow recapture of the USSR, forced the Germans to retreat from Ukraine and freed the capital, Kiev. But Ukrainian rebels ambushed him in February 1944, far from the front lines, and Nicolai Fyodorovich Vatutin died of his wounds.

GUEORGUI KONSTANTINOVITCH JUKOV, RUSSIAN GENERAL

A farmer's son, Gueorgui Konstantinovitch Jukov's youth was spent in the fields. However, his studies were not neglected and he was even found to be quite gifted. He became master furrier, a job that made it easier to survive in the poverty-ridden Russia of the beginning of the 20th century.

Enlisted during the First World War, he distinguished himself through his intelligence and became a sub-officer. But the horrors of the war and the hatred he felt towards his superiors convinced him to look for peace. Therefore, he became positively inclined to the Bolshevik Revolution in 1917 and obtained many victories during the subsequent civil war.

During the interwar period, he ascended through the military hierarchy and immediately joined the cavalry. Afterwards, Georgui Konstantinovitch Jukov became particularly interested in the panzer divisions, which he considered to be of paramount importance in modern warfare.

When Operation Barbarossa took the USSR by surprise, he was tasked with the defense of Ukraine against the German advance. His biggest success remains the defense of Moscow in 1941. Indeed, after the status quo between Japan and the USSR, he repatriated his elite troops from the east of the country and managed to save Moscow from a battle which already seemed to be lost.

In 1943, General Gueorgui Konstantinovich Jukov was the first to realize that the Germans would strike at Kursk, even before the Führer's approval of the operation. For this battle, he favored defense over attack and suggested fortifying the salient as much as possible. Moreover, he dissuaded Nikolai Fedorovitch Vatutin from attacking the Germans preventively, in order to spare the Russian forces. Nevertheless, he left the command of the operations to the latter.

At the end of the war, he was demoted by Stalin, who feared his popularity. Until his death, in 1974, he was mostly excluded from all political power, even though he was recognized as a war hero.

ANALYSIS OF THE BATTLE

PREPARATIONS

After the defeat of February 1943, Adolf Hitler needed a victory as spectacular as that of Stalingrad had been for the Soviets, in order to reassure the German people. The *Wehrmacht*, which seemed invincible until then, was facing its first major defeats. In Africa, the divisions of General Erwin Rommel (1891-1944) were retreating faced with the combined forces of the Americans and the British. In Southern Europe, the Allies could land in Italy at any moment. As for the Eastern Front, it had become completely unstable for the German army. Even though General Erich von Manstein took Kharkov (one of the biggest cities of the USSR) in March 1943, the Red Army kept the upper hand. Moreover, most of the German generals, and perhaps Adolf Hitler himself, considered Germany to have henceforth lost all chances of prevailing in the USSR.

Meanwhile, the Führer needed to avenge the USSR in order to strengthen his prestige. To do so, he chose Kursk. The city, which had been in the hands of the Germans since 1941, had been recaptured by the Soviets two years later, who then concentrated a large army there. Kursk had indeed been transformed into an advanced Russian base to facilitate the recapture of the Orel-Briansk region in the north-west, and of Ukraine in the south-west. Although the *Wehrmacht* managed to destroy this position, the German Chancellor weakened the USSR significantly and may have opened the way for a new attack on Moscow.

To achieve this objective, the Führer approved and launched the Citadel plan conceived by Erich von Manstein, which involved trapping the Russian forces through simultaneous action in the north and in the south. The Germans thus hoped to destroy the operational reserves of the enemy, whilst significantly reducing the size of the front. Adolf Hitler was persuaded that the operation would be a success, on condition that it be launched early enough.

The German fighting force in charge of taking Kursk was composed of:

- more than 900 000 soldiers;
- approximately 2 500 tanks – 3 000, according to the Soviets;
- approximately 10 000 artillery pieces;
- at least 2 000 planes.

Although these numbers seem impressive, the offensive capacities of the Germans had largely diminished in four years. The Germans and their allies had already lost 500 000 men since the beginning of the conflict, maybe even as many as 700 000. The total enlisting previously decided by Adolf Hitler replaced only half of the registered losses. However, he had no doubts as to the outcome of the battle, considering the number of troops and materials engaged: nearly half his panzer troops were sent to that front.

The planned attack was no surprise to the Russians who had discovered the Germans' plans long ago thanks to the spying network *Lucy*. The Red Army had therefore immediately prepared for the attack, and since March, the Russians had fortified Kursk's position; they dug thousands of kilometers of trenches, planted hundreds of thousands of mines and prepared thousands of positions for the artillery. In some places, the Russian defenses were spread over more than 150 kilometers. However, the Russian staff remained concerned: in the past, the German panzer divisions had gone through similar defenses without much difficulty. Some generals even wondered whether the Red Army would be better to strike first;

Also with the Russians, the means engaged were enormous and reserve troops were added, which brought the total of the Russian manpower to approximately:

- two million soldiers;
- 500 tanks;
- 20 000 artillery pieces;
- 2 700 planes.

Although the Russian troops were greater in number, the forces present were not necessarily imbalanced. Indeed, the *Wehrmacht* possessed a technological and tactical superiority.

However, not all the German generals were as confident as their Führer. Aerial photos showed the vastness of the Soviet defense, which led them to believe that the Russians had been prepared for an attack on Kursk. Despite this, the German commanding officer Walter Model asked the Führer to delay the attack in order to wait for the new tank models *Tiger*, *Panther* and the *Jagdpanzer Elefant*. He also argued that with the rain season, roads were impassable for the panzers. On the other hand, Erich von Manstein would have preferred to attack as quickly as possible, before Kursk became an unassailable position. In the end, Walter Model's supporters were listened to. The attack was thus delayed until the month of July, which left even more time for the Russians to prepare.

THE CLASH OF TANKS

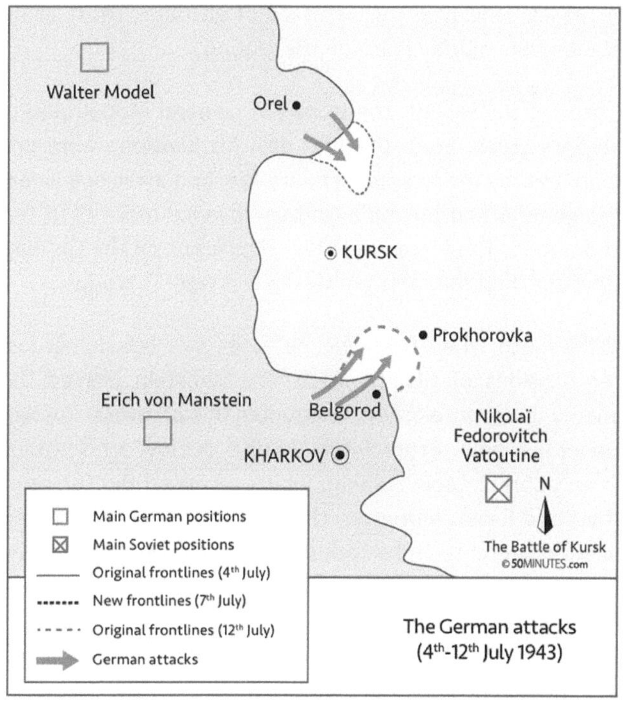

On 4 July 1943, the German army attacked the front posts in the south of Kursk. Each tank maneuver was preceded by an artillery barrage and an aerial bombing. But as the *Wehrmacht* didn't benefit from a surprise effect, it progressed with difficulty.

The next morning, the battlefield moved to the sky. To avoid being outflanked by the *Luftwaffe* (German aviation), the Russian air army engaged the fight and attacked the enemy air bases. However, through lack of gasoline, most of its planes were quickly stuck on the ground.

North of the salient, the troops of General Model quickly became stuck. From the first day, his divisions were immobilized by the Russian artillery fire, and after one week, the general had not managed to advance more than ten kilometers. The losses were less significant on the German side, but then they also possessed less reserve troops.

In the south, where the Soviet defenses were less numerous, the divisions of General Erich von Manstein pierced the enemy lines more easily. To counter this progress, Russian General Nikolai Fedorovitch Vatutin deployed his troops in an unpredictable fashion, which surprised the forces of the Third Reich. Moreover, the Russian general alternated between defense and attack strategies so as not to give the Germans one minute of rest. He also called many divisions as reinforcement and could rely on the Soviet sappers who, each night, placed mines on the path followed by the German tanks. This strategy gained results, with regards to the severe losses born by the *Wehrmacht*: after one week of fighting, some divisions were nearly annihilated. However, the Russian troops were not faring much better.

The culmination of the fighting took place on 12 and 13 July, with the Battle of the Prokhorovka (east of the Kursk salient), which is considered as the biggest tank battle in history. The tanks were so numerous that the aviation was incapable of distinguishing between the allied and enemy forces. However, aerial fighting remained of paramount importance to cover the tanks' progress; thus, both sides fought bitterly in the air.

This German breakthrough forced the Soviets to engage their reserve troops earlier than planned. Despite heavy losses, the *Wehrmacht* divisions still possessed 400 tanks. Soviet sources even mention 500 to 700 enemy tanks. These are mainly composed of three divisions of the *Waffen-SS*, the military branch of Hitler's elite troops: the 3rd division SS 'Totenkopf', the 2nd division 'Das Reich', and the 1st *Panzerkorps SS* 'Leibstandarte'. The Red Army operated 800 tanks, but their armor was much thinner.

Soviet tanks.

On 12 July, very early in the morning, the Germans engaged the hostilities at Prokhorovka, but the Soviet air forces quickly forced them to adopt a defensive position. The first Russian counter-attack was a disaster, particularly due to bad communication between the tanks and the planes. Decimated by the artillery, the frames of the Soviet tanks were on fire, reducing visibility on both sides. Therefore, the successive attacks of both the Germans and the Russians failed one after the other and the progress of the tanks was often impaired by air strikes on both sides. Moreover, these mechanized German divisions encountered a Soviet infantry which was well hidden behind its defenses. The losses, although unclear, were significant on both sides. Once more, the numerical superiority of the Russians made the difference in the end.

THE SOVIET COUNTER-ATTACK

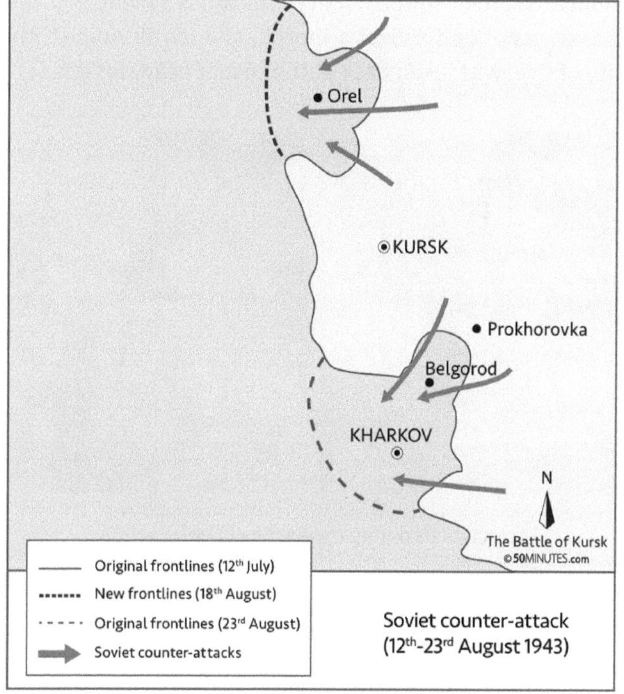

On 13 July, Adolf Hitler decided to abandon Operation Citadel. Not only had the German losses been very heavy, but the Allies had just landed in Sicily. The Führer was the-

refore forced to send a part of his troops to Italy in order to regain the upper hand. The eastern front was thus stripped to strengthen the German positions in Western Europe.

The Soviets took this opportunity to launch a counter-at-tack. From 12 July, the Red Army forced General Walter Model to retreat to the north of the Kursk salient. Fighting was to continue for over a month, and, on 18 August, the city of Orel was taken back at the cost of heavy losses.

Soviet troops during the Battle of Orel

In the South, the Russians took more time to reorganize: the Red Army had suffered the most losses there. Nevertheless, the Germans had also been pushed back. Although the Soviet forces marched towards Belgorod at the beginning of August, and took it easily, the recapture of Kharkov proved much more costly in lives. From 11-23 August, the German troops resisted bitterly on the front, but the *Wehrmacht* finally fell back behind the Dnieper (Eastern European River which ends in the Black Sea). With its victory at Kharkov, the Soviet Union shattered Adolf Hitler's last hopes: Nazi Germany would never triumph over the USSR. A preeminent industrial and strategic position, the city of Kharkov allowed the Russians to continue the attack towards the Dnieper, then Ukraine.

THE OUTCOME OF THE BATTLE: A FIELD OF BLOOD AND METAL

> "On 9 July, after four days of battle, anxiety was lessening; it diminished once it became known that 586 German tanks had been destroyed. [...] The press also published statements by astonished German prisoners: 'Never have we seen such a bloodbath among the German troops'" (Werth, 1964: 74).

After the Battle of Kursk, the German losses were indeed enough to affect troop morale. In a month and a half, more than half a million *Wehrmacht* soldiers were missing, either dead, wounded, or disappeared. Although the *Luftwaffe* did not suffer overly considerable losses, this was not the case with the German tanks: more than 1 200 tank frames were left behind on the Kursk salient. This was more than what they could produce.

Destroyed German tank.

For the Soviets, the battle was even more deadly. The Red Army counted more than 860 000 killed, wounded or missing. More than one thousand tanks and as many planes were destroyed. For their victory, the Soviet Union had thus sacrificed nearly half the troops present at Kursk.

REPERCUSSIONS OF THE BATTLE

ONE BATTLE, TWO PROPAGANDAS

As Hitler was counting on a victory in Kursk to boost the morale of the German population, the Führer preferred to remain silent on the significance of this defeat. In Berlin, Operation Citadel was almost forgotten from official statements, and although the propaganda tools happened to mention it, it was only to reduce its importance.

On the contrary, the Russian victory of Kursk was celebrated. The survivors of the battle were considered heroes and gave rise to many legends. For example, on 5 August 1943, at the liberation of Orel and Belgorod, Joseph Stalin congratulated his generals through the intermediary of Yuri Levitan (1914-1983), the star speaker of Radio-Moscow. The declaration was broadcast more than 300 times, until the final victory over Germany and Japan. On the same evening, the Russian capital echoed the 12 artillery salvos shot by 120 canons to salute the courage of the Soviet troops. The sky was also alight with the many fireworks reminding the population that the end of the war was now near.

THE SOVIET STEAMROLLER

For German historian Walter Gorlitz, "[Although] Stalingrad [was] the politico-psychological turning point of the war in the east, [...] the German defeat at Kursk and Belgorod [would be] the military turning point" (cited in Werth, 1954: p. 76).

Indeed, after the Battle of Kursk, the *Wehrmacht* would never again have the upper hand against the Red Army. From then on, the Germans would focus on strictly defensive actions, trying to avoid the inevitable. However, despite the failure of Operation Citadel, the *Wehrmacht* hoped to weaken the Russian forces enough to have time to reorganize. This was not so, as the Russians renewed their forces at an incredible pace. Reinforcements of men and materials kept streaming towards the front. Hence the expression "Soviet steamroller": the immensity of the Red Army crushed everything in its wake.

At the end of 1943, the Russians progressively liberated Ukraine, despite the brilliant tactical operations led by General Erich von Manstein. The following year, the Red Army broke the siege of Stalingrad and pursued its progress in Eastern Europe: Crimea, Belarus, Poland and the Balkans. After the capture of Austria, the Red Army was slowed down: the knowledge of the field played in the Germans' favor. However, the Soviets finally reached Berlin, which fell in April 1945 after the attack of 2.5 million soldiers. From the Battle of Kursk until the surrender on 7 May 1945, the Russian stranglehold never loosened on the Eastern Front.

THE SACRIFICES OF THE USSR

However, the Russian victory came at a price. The eastern front, the biggest theater of operations of the Second World War, was also the one which led to the most casualties. With 27 million killed, the Soviet Union alone registered the majority of losses on the side of the Allies, to which unfathomable material destructions were to be added: tens of thousands of cities and villages were destroyed.

However, by holding its own on the Eastern front, the USSR enabled the Allies to organize themselves and attack on several fronts. The Battle of Kursk therefore greatly facilitated the landing of the Americans and the British in Sicily (10 July 1943) and forced Germany to split up over several fronts in order to face the joint attacks of the Allies.

In the long term, the USSR's 'sacrifice' was therefore not in vain. The international position of the country was strengthened after the Second World War and, little by little, the countries of Eastern Europe fell within the influence sphere of Joseph Stalin. Thanks to his military and industrial power, the USSR became the world superpower which would frighten the whole world during the whole of the Cold War (1945-1990).

SUMMARY

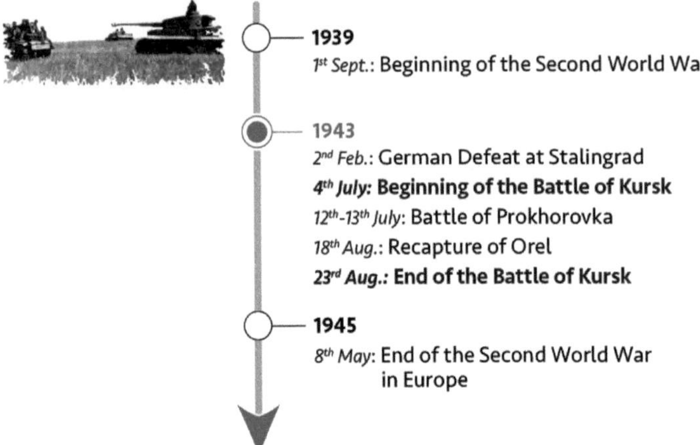

- In 1939, on the eve of the Second World War, Adolf Hitler and Joseph Stalin signed a pact of non-aggression. This meant that Germany and the USSR were to observe a strict neutrality if one of them were to be at war. The pact included a secret clause dividing the countries of Eastern Europe between them.

- Despite this pact of non-aggression, the Führer had always intended to invade the USSR, as, according to the Nazi doctrine, the Slavs were a race to be eliminated. It was for this reason that the Germans launched Operation Barbarossa in 1941, with the aim of overthrowing the communist regime. After a series of brilliant victories, Hitler's armed forces were stopped in Moscow, then in Stalingrad.

- After the defeat of Stalingrad at the beginning of 1943, the German chancellor wished to strike powerfully, in order to mark collective confidence. He decided to attack the Kursk salient, thanks to Operation Citadel. The aim was to catch the enemy in a vice-like grip, by attacking simultaneously from the north and the south. The goal was to destroy the strong concentration of Russian forces located there and to open the way to a new attack on Moscow.
- Foreseeing the attack, the Soviets fortified the Kursk salient for months. Mines were placed, thousands of kilometers of trenches were dug and hundreds of gun placements were scattered around. The Russians also planned for large amounts of reinforcement troops.
- On 4 July 1943, the Germans launched the attack. The fighting opposed millions of soldiers, thousands of tanks and planes, as well as tens of thousands of artillery pieces. At the beginning, the forces seemed to be balanced: while the Soviets were superior in number and had the advantage of the field, the Germans had the technological and tactical advantage.
- However, the German tanks quickly got bogged down in the north. In the south, the troops of General Erich von Manstein pierced the enemy lines more easily, but accumulated heavy losses due to the unpredictable strategy of the Russian General Nicolai Fyodorovich Vatutin.
- The fighting reached its peak on 12 July 1943, during the Battle of Prokhorovka. This was the biggest tank battle in history. There were such a large number of tanks that the aviation was unable to distinguish between the Allies and the enemies. Despite the heavy losses incurred on both

sides, the Soviet defenses held.

- The day after the battle, Adolf Hitler abandoned Operation Citadel. The losses were too extensive, and the Allies had just landed in Sicily. This was a military turning point: Hitler's Germany would never again have the upper hand over the USSR until the end of the war. Nothing could stop the 'Soviet Steamroller' on its way to Berlin.

FIND OUT MORE

BIBLIOGRAPHY

- Baechler, C. (2012) *Guerre et exterminations à l'Est. Hitler et la conquête de l'espace vital. 1933-1945*. Paris: Tallandier.
- Corelli, B. (1989) *Hitler's Generals*. New York: Grove Weidenfeld.
- Encyclopédie multimédia de la Shoah (No date) *L'Union Soviétique et le front de l'Est*. [Online] [Accessed 2 December 2016]. Available from: <http://www.ushmm.org/wlc/article.php?lang=fr&ModuleId=231>
- Husson, E., Werth, N. and Buffet, C. (2001) Hitler-Staline: la guerre à mort. *L'Histoire*, Volume 252.
- Kagan, F.W. (2002) The Great Patriotic War. In Higham, R. and Kagan, F.W. (eds.) *The Military History of the Soviet Union*. New York: Palgrave MacMillan, pp. 109-136.
- Laneyrie-Dagen, N. (2005) *Les grandes batailles de l'histoire*. Paris: Larousse.
- Lemay, B. (2006) *Erich von Manstein, le stratège d'Hitler*. Paris: Perrin.
- Mulligan, T.P. (1987) Spies, Ciphers and "Zitadelle": Intelligence and the Battle of Kursk, 1943. *Journal of Contemporary History*. 22(2), pp. 235-260.
- Quétel, C. (2007) *La Seconde Guerre mondiale*. Paris: Larousse.
- Savès, J. (2016) La Wehrmacht meurt une deuxième fois à Koursk. *Herodote.net*. [Online]. [Accessed 5 December 2016]. Available from: <https://www.herodote.net/5_juillet_1943-evenement-19430705.php>

* Shukman, H. (1993) *Stalin's generals*. New York: Phoenix.
* Werth, A. (1997) *Russia at War, 1941-45*. London, Carroll and Graf.

ADDITIONAL SOURCES

* Bartov, O. (1992) *Hitler's Army: Soldiers, Nazis and War in the Third Reich*. Oxford: Oxford University Press.
* Carell, P. (1994) *Scorched Earth: Russian-German War, 1943-1944*. Pennsylvania: Schiffer Publishing Ltd.
* Clark, L. (2012) *Kursk: The Greatest Battle*. London: Headline Publishing Group.
* Glantz, D.M. and House, J.M. (1999) *The Battle of Kursk*. Kansas: University Press of Kansas.
* Jukes, G. (1969) *Kursk: The Clash of Armour*. New York: Ballantine Books.
* Jukes, G. (2011) *Stalingrad to Kursk: Triumph of the Red Army*. Barnsley: Pen and Sword Military.
* Merridale, C. (2006) *Ivan's War: Inside the Red Army 1939-1945*. London: Faber and Faber Limited.

ICONOGRAPHIC SOURCES

* Soviet tanks. Royalty-free reproduction picture.
* Soviet troops during the Battle of Orel. Royalty-free reproduction picture.
* Destroyed German tank. Royalty-free reproduction picture.

DOCUMENTARIES

- *Images de la Seconde Guerre mondiale: La bataille de Koursk.* (2006) [Documentary]. Getty Hulton.
- *La Bataille de Koursk. La Terrible Défaite d'Hitler.* (2008) [Documentary]. Garofalo and Jeremy Joseph. Dir. France: Epi Diffusion.
- *La Bataille de Koursk. July 1943.* (2012) [Documentary]. Bundesarchiv.

MUSEUMS AND COMMEMORATIVE BUILDINGS

- Peter and Paul Cathedral, built on the battlefield of Prokhorovka (Russia).
- The obelisk of Prokhorovka (Russia).
- The Museum-diorama of the Battle of Kursk in Belgorod (Russia).